Walking through the Garden

By

Janie Cannon

© 2004 by Janie Cannon. All rights reserved.

No part of this book may be reproduced, stored in a retrieval system, or transmitted by any means, electronic, mechanical, photocopying, recording, or otherwise, without written permission from the author.

First published by AuthorHouse 04/26/04

ISBN: 1-4184-5650-0 (e-book)
ISBN: 1-4184-3661-5 (Paperback)

This book is printed on acid free paper.

Introduction

As you walk through this garden of verse, may you find peace, joy, and serenity of Spirit. Life today offers so many serious challenges. There seems to be a countless multitude of negative events occurring moment by moment, day after day. Please join me now in this quiet walk; and let us experience, together, the positive and spiritual adventure that awaits us.

Each of us may, at some time, feel the need to enter a small avenue of escape. We need to temporarily wander away from it all; to cross over to a place of blessed assurance, that will ignite a brand new awakening.

My ultimate desire is to enhance a portion of spiritual strength and healing for everyone who begins this journey with me. May all of the positive thoughts that you share here continue to follow you as you walk forward through the garden of life. May your souls become intensely enriched for having passed this way.

Dedication of Book

I dedicate this book of spiritual prose to my four married children and their spouses. Also, to my grandchildren and to my great grandchildren.

Whenever I've attempted to accomplish anything, I can thank God that I've always had my four children to encourage me. Whenever a crisis occurred in my life, they were there eager to assist me both financially and emotionally. To God be the glory for having loaned them to me. Without their support, and the goodness and mercy of the almighty God, could I have completed this task? I think not. God is truly good and worthy to be praised.

I have a host of friends, both old and young, whom I have come to love dearly over the past years. They are all very special people in my life and mean a great deal to me. I do not even have enough room to include all of their names but they are written in my heart and spirit and they know "who they are".

Listings

Introduction..iii

Dedication of Book..v

Listings vii

Through the Garden...ix

Spread a little Joy..1

Who will answer for you?...3

Did you lend a Helping Hand 5

A Charge to keep for Christ...7

If Jesus walks beside Us 9

Go Your Way...11

Where does the sunset Go?..13

Christian Brotherhood 15

The Day of the Saints is Upon Us 17

I wonder what heaven is Like..19

When Sorrow comes..21

Behold the Bridegroom cometh...23

Closeness with Jesus...25

Completing God's plan...27

What is a world without God?	29
Christ is always the same	31
Greed	33
The Joy of Jesus	35
Little things Mean a Lot	37
Give praise	39
If we only learn to wait	41
Just before the Blessings	43
Love Is	45
The Great Shepherd	47
About the Author	49

Psalms 91:1 "He that dwelleth in the Secret Place of the Most High shall abide under the shadow of the, Almighty

Through the Garden

As I walk through the garden

I feel his presence near

T' is great to feel the closeness

That casts away all fear.

As I walk through the garden

I never feel alone

He supplements my spirit

And gives my heart a song.

As I walk through the garden

sometimes the billows rise

Would I but flinch or ponder

But into his arms I hide

As I walk through the garden

The dew is gently thrown

the wetness purely intercedes

The joy of our celestial home.

As I walk through the garden

My heavenly father greets me there

I find such peace and loving grace

As I linger in his care.

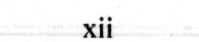

Walking through the Garden

Neh. 8:10 "For the Joy of the Lord is your strength"

Spread a little Joy

Spread a little joy each day

A gift, a smile, a touch

A word of real encouragement

Can mean so very much

To heal a broken hearted soul

To lift a spirit depressed

May gain much happiness with-in

And cause you to be blessed

Spread a little joy wherever you go

Dismantle all meanness and pride

Do not concentrate on negative thoughts

Just continue on the positive side.

Janie Cannon

The World has it's share of gloom and woe

We all have our crosses to bare

But kindness and love may heal a wound

Allowing others to feel our care.

Spread a little Joy wherever you go

Follow the savior's plan in all that you do

Just give to the world your very best

And the joy of Jesus will follow you.

Walking through the Garden

Rev 21: 7 "He that overcometh shall inherit all things; and I will be his God, and he shall be my son."

Who will answer for you?

When the roll is called in heaven

And the saints go marching through

Brother, Who will shout at your attendance

Oh, who will answer for you?

In the great and final day of judgment

And there's no more left to do

Sister, who will meet your master face to face?

Oh, who will answer for you?

When Jesus says "Time will be no more"

As the saints are made anew

Preacher, who will give God your final praise

Oh, who will answer for you?

Janie Cannon

In that sweet and final "Bye and Bye"

As we greet the Savior kind and true

Christian, who will shout your last "Hallelujah"?

Your life of "Holiness" must answer for you.

He continues to stand with outstretched arms

Reaching down from heaven above

And He remains ever ready to greet me

into this beautiful garden of love.

Walking through the Garden

Proverbs 3:27

"Withhold no good from them to whom it is due, When it is in the power of thine hand to do it."

Did you lend a Helping Hand

Did you stop to extend your hand today

Did you anchor a ship that has gone astray

Did you wipe a tear as you knelt to pray

Did you lend a helping hand

Did you offer a garment to a needy friend

Did you try to pursue his soul to win

Are you fasting and praying "now and then"

Did you lend a helping hand.

Janie Cannon

When you visited the sick as they lay in bed

Did you refrain from gossip, but served them instead

Did you see that they were being properly fed

Did you lend a helping hand

As you wander through life while doing God's deeds

Do you try to give freely and serve unattended needs

By reaching out to others and answering their pleas

Did you lend a helping hand?

Walking through the Garden

Psalm 91:11 "He shall give His angels charge over thee, to keep thee in all thy ways"

A Charge to keep for Christ

We have a charge to keep for Christ, to serve him everyday

To live a life of holiness in every Godly way

When we were saved we made the vow to serve him, without sin

We shouldn't forget the charge we made; to follow it to the end.

We have a charge to keep for Christ to praise him day by day

To tell the world about his goodness, and never from his paths to stray

To find the lost and forlorn souls to aid those in distress

To help those who seek redemption and God's spirit of righteousness

We have a charge to keep for Christ, there's so much trouble and ruin

We need to do our best each day for we know not when he will return

There's sickness and sorrow throughout the land, disasters every day

More family commitments on the brink, bringing misery in every way

Janie Cannon

We have a charge to keep for Christ, he's always standing near

Beckoning," Come unto me all ye that labor." Then he removes the

fear

We have the assurance of this king that our battle is already won

It's easy to conquer our enemies, when we trust his "Begotten" Son.

We have a charge to keep for Christ through the valleys and hills of

life

Though the roads are rocky and the journey long, we must make the

sacrifice.

Our sacrifice is our charge to keep, our vow "to praise," not to mourn

And to keep our focus on heavenly things till our Saviour takes us

home.

Walking through the Garden

John 14:6 Jesus saith, I am the way, the truth, and the life: no man cometh unto the Father, but by me

If Jesus walks beside Us

If Jesus walks beside us, we cannot fail the test

Though life's darts strike, they bounce right back

And keep our minds at rest.

If Jesus walks beside us, our lives are in control

We lean on his power, during every hour

As life's billows burst and roll

If Jesus walks beside us, We'll love him more and more

He's always there, He'll always care.

Through rugged mountains He'll guide us o're.

If Jesus walks beside us, our way is clear and real

His love shines bright, he guides the night

With God like mercy and zeal.

Janie Cannon

If Jesus walks beside us each minute and every hour.

He'll extend his love, from his throne above

And give us his spiritual power.

If Jesus walks beside us, and we give him our lives to restore

He'll save us today, He'll come in to stay

And we can join hands with him forever more.

Walking through the Garden

Matt 12:35 "A good man out of the good treasure of the heart bringeth forth good things."

Go Your Way

Go your way and tell the world about Jesus

Tell them how he set you free

Tell them how he gave his life so eagerly

Just to salvage you and me.

Go your way and mention "power"

Jesus gives it to saints who are bold

Power to pray and to cast out demons

Power to heal the sin sick soul.

Go your way and mention "Gladness"

'I was glad ", said brother David, "when they said"

"Let us go into the house of prayer"

For there we will receive our daily bread

Janie Cannon

Go your way and mention "mansions"

Jesus promised them as our future site

They who follow in his footsteps

They who love Jesus and live right

Go your way and mention "friendship"

Jesus is our closest friend

If we only love and trust him

He'll protect us until the end

Walking through the Garden

Psalm 128:1 "Blessed is every one that feareth the Lord, that walketh in his ways"

Where does the sunset Go?

Where does the sunset go at the close of the day.

Rolling around to other shores in awesome array

Silently I stood and watched as it weakened it's shine

Such a bright and glorious element of the great divine

Where does the sunset go, I was playing chance

Then I looked beyond the hills and bright rays seemed to dance.

Gone was that glorious light made for family frolic

Gone was the brightness of another melancholic

Where does the sunset go; as it moves in quick pace

No time to fool around and little time to waste

Tasks not in order, so much work to do

Before I realize it another day has passed through.

Janie Cannon

Where does the sunset go I see it o'er the border

Reminds me, as a Christian, to get my life in order

So that at my last sunset when I must thus "join in"

I'll follow it with Christ on that great judgment morning.

Walking through the Garden

Romans 12:5 For we, being many are

one body in Christ."

Christian Brotherhood

We need true Christian Brotherhood

Among our neighbors, among our folk

Among our churches, among our citizens

Throughout the world from coast to coast.

We need to help our fellowmen in times of trouble

And comfort friends in their despair

To let them know we are our brother's keeper

Who feel another brother's care.

We need to help the suffering widow

To see that the fatherless child has a friend

To lift our hand to a drunken sinner

And try for the master his soul to win

Janie Cannon

To visit the sick in their painful moments

And utter for them an humble prayer

That God will have mercy and touch their bodies

And keep them in his loving care

We need to remember the ones in need of shelter

And assist them in their time of strife

That we, through this small Christian gesture

Will reflect God's mercy on our own life.

We know we can't do all for others

Our capacity of humanity may be narrow and slight

But surely the least we do for Jesus

Will "forever" be "precious" in his sight.

Walking through the Garden

Rev. 2:26 He that overcometh,

and keepeth my works

unto the end to him will

I give power over the nations

The Day of the Saints is Upon Us

The Day of the saints is upon us

The blessing are here to receive

The power of God's spirit surrounds us

It's time for us to believe.

Believe in King Jesus our Redeemer

Believe that he died for our sins

That he is soon coming back to receive us

And take us to his kingdom within.

Janie Cannon

For didn't he promise to save us?

And doesn't the bible speak true'

And isn't he the great "Lords of Lords"

Who maketh his works known to you

The day of the saints is upon us

The blessings are here to behold

The savior is pleading and beckoning

Reach Out! Touch! And be more whole!

Walking through the Garden

Rev. 21:2 I John *saw the new Jerusalem, coming down from God*

prepared as a bride

I wonder what heaven is Like

As I sit today and ponder and look towards the celestial shore

I think about the horizons of the land of "evermore"

I see the blazing sunshine as it's light rays cover the sound

And wonder about the great place of super awesome renown.

They say there no more sickness, for death there has lost it's "root"

I wonder about the streets of gold and the trees of "healing" fruit

I consider the rocks of ages and the valley of joy to behold.

And know that my savior awaits me with chariots of solid gold.

As I sit here today and wonder about that city, none can compare

So many things excite me so many expectations up there

I wonder about the twelve gates and the guards who stand" about

face"

Janie Cannon

I wonder how they must have sacrificed to come to such a "credible"

place.

I wonder what heaven s really like, who's cleaning the pearly streets?

Are they washed daily by the radiance of the elect's sanctified feet?

Who is cleaning the emerald mansion that gleams in constant array?

Contrasting the fervent glitter from the praises of saints day by day

I wonder how the big city is, the bible says there's room for all

Of those who love him and live holy, and never ignore his call

I'd just like to know what heaven is like, I'm curious and sometimes I

sigh

So I must live holy, loving, and merciful, and I'll find the answer by

and by.

Walking through the Garden

Matt. 11:28 "Come unto me, All ye that labor and are heavy laden, and I will give you rest."

When Sorrow comes

When sorrow comes into our lives

We have to pause for awhile

It may be the loss of someone we love

Or a disobedient child.

It may be a spouse who is following sin

And running to and fro

It may be the secret inward hurts

For reasons that we don't seem to show.

Perhaps a dear and loving friend

Has turned away from us

And hasn't bothered to explain

His silence or disgust.

Janie Cannon

We may find that our joy subsides

As sorrows fill our mind

But we can go to God in prayer

And seek his peace divine.

When sorrow comes into our life.

And one day it will so do

We have a hope in Christ the King

Who'll be there to see us through

Walking through the Garden

Isaiah 62:5 "As the Bridegroom rejoiceth on the bride, as shall thy God rejoice over thee

Behold the Bridegroom cometh

Behold the Bridegroom cometh

To claim his faithful bride

Will we run to greet his outstretched arms

Or will we try to hide.

He is coming to gather his loving saints

And end their struggle and snare

Will we say to him "we've followed the cross"

Or will we be left in despair?

Oh when He comes to carry us

To that everlasting shore

Will we mount up as doves ascending

Or be doomed forevermore

Janie Cannon

Behold the bridegroom cometh

And nobody knows just how soon

But if we live holy according to his word

We will someday join our eternal groom,

Walking through the Garden

Prov. 18:24 "There is a friend who sticks closer than a brother"

Closeness with Jesus

Closeness with Jesus come what may

I need to get closer every day

There is no time to ponder no time to stray

The storms are raging across the bay.

Closeness with Jesus I seek his peace

I need to gain more spiritual relief

I need to create a prayerful feast

T'will grant me a merciful gracious release.

Closeness with Jesus I need to abide

Safe in his bosom just to sweetly hide

All my secret thoughts with him I will confide

While with him daily side by side.

Janie Cannon

Closeness with Jesus till this is o're

Then he'll safely guide to the other shore

To the home prepared for me through an open door

Inside that great land of "Evermore".

Walking through the Garden

Ps 20:4 "May he give you the desire of your heart, and make all your plans succeed"

Completing God's plan

The organ is playing the choir is swaying

A beautiful sound heard near

The bells are ringing the birds are singing

God's plan for your life is made clear.

You've worked and you've sweated, you've never once fretted

Each trial brings you closer to home

For life is a struggle and through every huddle

You know that you're never alone.

Your faith is now growing and bright skies are glowing

For time is still on your side

Each days seems unclear, less hope and more fear

So you seek more in Christ to confide.

Janie Cannon

In all your tomorrows he'll still bear your sorrows

And withhold you so that you will stand

Till you gain your destiny and claim total victory

Then you'll know you've completed God's plan.

Walking through the Garden

Ps 18:2 "The Lord is my rock, my fortress, my deliverer, my God, my strength, my buckler, the horn of my salvation, and my high tower.

What is a world without God?

What is a home without a mother?

What is stress without strife?

What is a sister without a brother?

What is breathe without life?

What is battle without a conflict?

What is brawn without a brain?

What is work without labor?

What is success without pain?

What is money without power?

What is grief without despair?

What is joy without happiness?

What is toil without snare?

Janie Cannon

What is a soul without a savior?

What is faith without hope?

What is peace without conflict?

What is purpose without scope?

What is life without the living?

What is a seed without a pod?

What is love without a love one?

What is a world without God?

Walking through the Garden

1st Peter 4:14 "If ye be reproached for the name of Christ, happy are ye."

Christ is always the same

Christ is always just the same and he never changeth

Through all time he will remain as he ever reigneth

Yesterday he came to man, born inside a manger.

With all power in his hand surrounded by millions of angels

Walked among the sons of men saved and healed his brother

Died to fulfill righteousness, loved us like no other.

Now He's still among the saints, beckoning us to follow

Faithfully trusting through his grace lessens all our sorrow

Thus we feel his precious power in our gains and losses

Helping us gently hour by hour as we endure our crosses

Each day we know, if we live right, his strong hands are waiting

Eyes of pity, arms of love, lends no hesitating.

Janie Cannon

Christ is always just the same, leading to perfection

Encircling his love around our lives filled with firm protection

He's the friend who'll grasp us close as we reach the border

If we've lived a sanctified life we become immortal

Thus to live always with him free and purified

As He, the great unchangeable one, forever will abide

Walking through the Garden

Prov 15:27 "He that is greedy of gain troubleth his own house; but he that hateth gifts shall live"

Greed

Greed is the love of worldly things

More than the love of God

Greed is the lust of life's riches

And the willingness to obtain them by fraud.

Greed is the selfishness that enters the heart

And always seeks "more and more"

He's never satisfied with a piece of the "lot"

But he aims to acquire the "whole floor"

Greed is the gullible spirit of desire

"Can't stop" till you've grabbed it all

No concern for others while reaching out

Nor caring about who stumbles or falls.

Janie Cannon

Greed may be the downfall of many of us

Who profess to claim God's Word indeed

With greed on board there's never enough room

To befriend those who may be in need.

Greed must go and love must come

If Christ's spirit is to thrive within you

Aid graciously, give abundantly and live holy each day

Destroying greed as God's love comes in view.

Walking through the Garden

Neh. 8:10 "The joy of the Lord is your strength."

The Joy of Jesus

The Joy of Jesus is our strength

It guides from day to day

It leads our footsteps as we trod

Along the narrow way

It helps us climb the rugged hills

Or sink through valleys scope

When 'ere we're down it lifts us up

And gives our spirit hope

The Joy of Jesus takes us through

Each long and stormy stand

Our life exalts a blessed peace

If joy is in the plan

Janie Cannon

Life has it's share of ups and downs

Some good, some bad, tis true

But know that Jesus holds that joy

And it will see us through

Walking through the Garden

Ps 10:17 "Lord thou hast heard the desire of the humble: thou wilt prepare their heart;"

Little things Mean a Lot

For every day in every way

Little things mean a lot

Throughout the years, during strife and tears

Little things mean a lot.

When things go wrong and there's no song

Little things mean a lot

When things are fair, and you can share

Little things mean a lot.

When friends asunder and one may wonder

Little things mean a lot

We're often mistaken and feel forsaken

Little things mean a lot.

Janie Cannon

We seek the savior and plead his favor

Little things mean a lot

He won't forsake us when trouble overtakes us

Little things mean a lot.

His grace is descending and never ending

Little things mean a lot

His love is sharing forever caring

Little things mean a lot.

Walking through the Garden

Ps. 7:17 "I will sing praise to the name of the Lord most high"

Give praise

Give praise for the rising of the morning sun

Give praise for the holy one

Give praise for the clouds whether blue or gray

Give praise for the start of another day.

Give praise when you look in the eyes of your child

Give praise as God blesses you all the while

Give praises for tiny feet and the cute impish way

Give praise for the greatness of a future day.

Give praise for the spouse God gave you to share

Give praise through life's problem that come "here" and "there"

Give praise as Christ keeps fulfilling your dream

Give praise as your Christian commitments are esteemed.

Janie Cannon

Give praise for the creature, the birds and bees

Give praise for the beautiful flowers and trees

Give praise for the weeds, some are helpful to man

Give praise for their special role in God's plan.

Give praise everyday just for being alive

Give praise as you know you have Christ on your side

Give praise, many praises; in all that you do

Give praise and great blessings will come back to you.

Walking through the Garden

Is. 40:31 "They that wait upon the Lord shall renew their strength"

If we only learn to wait

Life could be different and well understood

And many sorrows we could negate

Things that are crucial may thus be made good

If we only learn to wait.

Life has it's own way of settling the score

Though it seems to move in slow pace

God has promised to open every door

If we only learn to wait.

What is life without its ups and downs

Some consider it pure luck or fate

Whatever we encounter, our goals will be found

If we only learn to wait.

Janie Cannon

Sound out good ideas, put them in view

Work towards them don't hesitate

We'll conquer, we'll succeed, in whatever we do.

If we only learn to wait

Walking through the Garden

Psalms 34:19 "Many are

the afflictions of the righteous;

But the Lord delivereth him

out of them all

Just before the Blessings

Just before the blessings we face the storm

Billows roll and fierce winds are formed

Just before the blessings we shun the blast

Satan's darts pierce us strong and fast.

Just before the blessings we walk alone

Friends depart leaving us powerless and forlorn

Just before the blessings we feel the thorn

Hope diminished and prosperity gone.

Just before the blessings we reach despair

WE seek our precious Savior to grasp his love and care

Janie Cannon

Just before the blessings we look to the mountain

And reach upward to touch the eternal fountain

Just before the blessings we know we've been tried

WE then realize our need to allow God to abide,

Just before the blessings we hear him say

"Take hold of my hand and I'll lead the way".

Just before the blessings we feel his touch from above

God is just about to expand his goodness and love

Just before the blessings we've passed the test we know

As his everlasting mercy continues to grow and grow.

Walking through the Garden

Jer. 31:3 "I have loved these with an everlasting love."

Love Is

Love is giving to all in need as much as your profits allow

Love is planting a Godly seed and nurturing it with nuzzle and plow.

Love is suffering, being kind, envying no other man

Love is humbleness, letting God's light shine, and living within His plan.

Love is hoping, rejoicing in faith and striving to win souls each day

Love is knowledge to live for Christ, helping others along the way.

Love is abandoning evil thoughts and evil deeds of sin

Love is the grasp "Godly" things, in order to "make it in".

Love is in the final *BIG* triangle: **Holy Ghost, Father, and Son.**

Love is Knowing that this **TRINITY** is really "Three in One".

Janie Cannon

Love is the power he has given the world, "to be saved ye must believe"

Love is the end result of *His* love, "If we believe we shall receive".

Walking through the Garden

Psalms 23:1

"the Lord is My Shepherd

I shall not want."

The Great Shepherd

The great shepherd is Jesus our savior and friend

Only he will deliver us at life's final end.

He'll walk with us daily, he'll guide us along.

He'll help us realize the right from the wrong.

When life gets overburdened and friends disappear

The great shepherd, our savior, will become "ere" so near.

When sadness envelopes, or finances fall through

Jesus, the true shepherd, sups at the table with you.

Janie Cannon

We weren't promised life without obstacles or pain

Nor joyous days always, or sun without rain.

But the good shepherd continues to be true to his plan

In time he lifts the gray clouds and heals the land.

We never have to worry about unknown fear

As long as we're assured that he's ever near.

Acknowledge the Great Shepherd and study his ways

He'll then guide our pathways throughout all our days.

And at last when we have run this race and "stood the test"

Our Great Shepherd will take us to his "mission of rest".

About the Author

Ms Cannon, a widow since 1984, is a mother, grandmother and great grandmother. She has written poetry since her early childhood years, continuously sharing them with schools, churches, civic groups and friends. Her poetry consists of "spiritual", "inspirational" and "children" poems.

She received a Bachelors degree as a Liberal Arts Major from Adelphi University. During her lifetime, she has held many positions. She has always considered herself as a "career" woman. Even now, at the age of "retirement", she finds time to volunteer her services throughout her neighborhood whenever she sees the need.

Her greatest desire, at the present time, is to be a real source of inspiration to her children, grandchildren, and to all of her wonderful friends who share this experience with her. She wants to spread her positive notions; that life is full of great surprises and positive ideas. One needs only to tread forward and explore the challenge.